LATERAL THINKING PUZZLES & PARADOXES

THIS IS A CARLTON BOOK

Published in 2016 by Carlton Books Limited
an imprint of the Carlton Publishing Group
20 Mortimer Street
London W1T 3JW

A catalogue record for this book is available from the
British Library

ISBN 978-1-78097-831-4

Printed in Dubai

10 9 8 7 6 5 4 3 2 1

LATERAL THINKING PUZZLES & PARADOXES

MORE THAN **90** BRAINTEASERS
TO SOLVE WITH LOGICAL REASONING

ERWIN BRECHER, PhD

CARLTON
BOOKS

CONTENTS

ABOUT THE AUTHOR

Erwin Brecher was educated in Vienna, Czechoslovakia and London. He studied physics, economics and engineering to become AMIMechE and AMIProdE. For his PhD, he majored in psychology. Brecher joined the Czech army in 1937, and at the outbreak of war escaped to London via Switzerland. He worked for De Havilland on aircraft design, and in 1946 formed a group of companies active in international trade and finance. In 1963 his companies were acquired by a listed investment trust. He was appointed to the main board and to the board of its banking subsidiary. In 1972 Erwin Brecher became CEO of an international financial group with offices in New York, Rio de Janeiro, Switzerland, Athens and Istanbul. He specialized in developing a technique known as International Counter-trade in connection with which he travelled extensively. In 1974 he became a Name at Lloyds of London. Then in 1978, he acquired control of a quoted investment trust and served as its chairman until his retirement in 1984. Erwin Brecher was a shareholder and on the board of MBA International, a specialist recruitment company. He was also CEO of a company of financial consultants (established in 1947).

He was the author of many books on non-fiction subjects, published in six languages by US and European companies. In September 1995 he was awarded the Order of Merit in Gold by the city of Vienna in recognition of his literary achievements.

Erwin Brecher was a member of Mensa and has been a regular contributor to magazines and radio in the UK and abroad.

INTRODUCTION

This book deals with a novel and exciting approach to puzzle-solving, describing situations which appear unusual and even weird, defying any attempt to find a ready explanation. However, the puzzles are constructed in a manner which will make the circumstances fit one reasonable and logical answer. Each puzzle contains, in addition to irrelevancies, all necessary ingredients to satisfy the solution.

While solving these puzzles is usually quite tough, creating new ones along similar lines need not be, once players have developed an understanding of what makes them tick. Devotees should therefore be able to keep the parlour game going after the examples provided in this book are exhausted. Indeed I am looking forward to a flood of ideas from my readers, which will be gratefully acknowledged.

Strange situations, by their very nature, appear to provide the possibility of more than just one correct answer. Indeed, at first glance they might seem to offer an almost infinite number of solutions, limited only by the breadth of the solver's imagination. Certainly, they do not have mathematically definitive answers in the way that conventional puzzles do; but in my experience, on both sides of the fence, there is usually only one solution – ignoring minor variations of detail – that both puzzler and responder find correct and satisfactory. Substantially different alternatives tend to seem second-rate, even to the answerers who devized them, once the "official" answer is known.

As to the technique of interrogation, finding the solution requires a radically different thought process from the standard puzzle. The issues in most conventional brain-teasers are self-evident; they jump out at the puzzler and trigger the thought processes, leading in a direction (which may turn out to be right or wrong). For instance, if a problem requires calculation with pen and paper, the puzzler is usually able to begin the figure work and put pen to paper as soon as he or she has finished reading it. This is not the case with the problems in this book. They are conundrums in which half the battle is figuring out where to begin and which piece of given information is the key to unravelling the mystery. They test a kind of cross between lateral and intuitive thinking rather than mechanical intelligence, numeracy or acquired knowledge.

The problems are generally in the form of a narrative, telling a story that seems out of kilter in some way. It may seem wildly improbable or contradictory; it may describe bizarre or otherwise inexplicable conduct; it may even seem to defy the laws of physics! But there is a rational explanation for the story and the object of the puzzle is to find that explanation.

The ground rules are as follows: The solution must obviously fit all the given facts, must conform to accepted norms of behaviour and obey the laws of the physical world as we know it; in other words, you can take it for granted that none of the solutions involves women from Mars who can fly and see through concrete.

Having said that, perhaps I should add one thing. By "rational explanation" I do not mean to suggest that the situations, once explained, will all seem realistic in everyday-world terms, merely that they will suddenly make sense according to the puzzler's concept of acceptable logic.

PLAYING AS A GAME

Although you can of course tackle these problems on your own, they can also be great fun as a parlour game, which is best played with a moderator who knows the answer, and one or several participants who can ask any number of questions which the moderator can only answer with "Yes" or "No" until one of the players has found the solution. A useful refinement is to add "Irrelevant" to the moderator's responses, as many questions cannot be answered with "Yes" or "No" and to do so would only confuse the questioner. As an alternative to one or more individuals playing the game, the participants (if more than three) can split into two groups, who are permitted to consult among themselves.

There are many puzzles with complex solutions, which can be arrived at only in stages, in which case the participants profit substantially from questions and answers of competitors. It is therefore advizable to base the scoring on an aggregate of questions yielding a "Yes" response and awarding bonus points to the group, which articulates the correct solution. Two points are awarded for asking a correct question about the background and 10 points for finding the solution. If just one person is playing alone, then take away 1 point for each question asked, right or wrong, but give 20 points for the correct answer.

The key to success is an intelligent and methodical approach to formulating questions, which should be designed to narrow the field in successive steps, almost like a forensic exercise.

Let us take one of the classic riddles and see how it works:

A banker lives on the twentieth floor of a high-rise apartment building in Manhattan. Each morning when he goes to work he calls the lift, pushes the ground-floor button and is driven by chauffeured limousine to his Wall Street office.

On his return home he enters the lift, usually pushes the twelfth-floor button and walks up the rest of the stairs. At other times he rides straight up to his floor.

Question – Why does he not always take the lift to the twentieth floor?

Assuming two teams, Team A and Team B, the game and the scoring might develop something like this:

> **Team A**: Is there a regular pattern in the banker's behaviour?
> Answer: No.
> **Team B**: Does he walk up for exercise?
> Answer: No.
> **Team A**: Does he occasionally visit someone on the twelfth floor? Answer: No.
> **Team B**: Is his behaviour random?
> Answer: No.
> **Team A**: Is going to the twelfth or twentieth floor conditional on extraneous circumstances?
> Answer: Yes, +2 Bonus Points.

Team B: Are other people involved in his decision?
Answer: Yes, +2 Bonus Points.
Team A: Are these people also travelling in the lift with him? Answer: Yes, +2 Bonus Points.
Team B: Are the other passengers also stopping on the twelfth floor? Answer: Irrelevant.
Team A: Does he stop at the twelfth floor only if there are no other passengers in the lift?
Answer: Yes, +2 Bonus Points.
Team B: Is he disabled?
Answer: No.
Team A: Is he for any reason unable to operate the twentieth-floor button?
Answer: Yes, + 2 Bonus Points.
Team B: Is he very short?
Answer: Yes, 10 points.
Team B wins by 12 points to 8.

PUZZLES

MYOPIA

Albert Grey was severely myopic (short-sighted) from birth. In fact the vision test he had to undergo produced results which brought into question whether he would qualify for a driving licence. After an appeal he was issued a licence on the condition that he would always wear appropriate spectacles.

One very sunny day on a shopping trip he wore his optical sunglasses which fully conformed with the condition imposed on him. On his return trip he collided with another car. A policeman who witnessed the accident was first of the opinion that the other driver was at fault and reported accordingly. But he also noticed that Albert Grey was not wearing any glasses, as stipulated in the driving licence. When challenged on this point, Albert showed the PC a piece of paper which resolved the issue.

What was it?

THE TELEPHONE
CONVERSATION

"Hello, is that 966 9876?"

"Yes it is, who's that calling?"

"Don't you recognize my voice? You should, my mother is your mother's mother-in-law."

"Eh?"

Who was having a telephone conversation?

THE MENU

A well-dressed couple enter a sumptuous restaurant in midtown Manhattan. They ask for the menu and wine list, which they study intently. They then order cocktails and place their order for a four-course dinner. As they enjoy their drinks, they engage in animated conversation. Suddenly the man looks at his watch and the couwple get up and leave hurriedly, without waiting for the meal.

The Maitre D' watches them leave, but makes no attempt to question or stop them.

Explain.

DISCERNING
SHOPPER

A woman is seen pushing a shopping cart around a large grocery store just before closing time. She stops at various points, carefully selects items and loads them into the cart. When she is finished, she leaves the store. However, she does not pass through the checkout, nor does she pay for any of the items she has selected.

Explain.

PERIL IN THE AIR

On a scheduled flight from Istanbul to New York an incident occurred which will be remembered for a long time by the passengers. During the flight, a first-class passenger suddenly disappeared from the plane. He did not jump out, nor did anyone push him. In fact, the doors of the plane were closed and secured at the time of the disappearance. Yet his shattered body was discovered elsewhere a few days later. What had happened?

THE VERDICT

The trial had been a lengthy one. George Bishop had been accused of premeditated murder. The jury had taken hours to reach their verdict but now they had finally returned.

The judge asked them if they had reached a unanimous verdict, and they replied that they had. The accused was then released, although the jury had not found him
"Not Guilty".

Explain.

THE VANDAL

A rough-looking stranger enters a restaurant with a sledgehammer. He selects one of two identical pieces of equipment and, without warning, smashes it into fragments. He then walks out without uttering a word.

The restaurant owner is not surprised. In fact, he seems to have expected the visit and makes no attempt to interfere. However, after the visitor leaves, the owner makes one telephone call, as a result of which the body of the stranger is discovered next morning in a ditch outside town.

What has happened?

JEALOUSY

A circus troupe is like a large family, and many of the famous names of travelling showmen of the fairgrounds have become part of "Big Top" folklore, to be remembered by children of all ages and never to be forgotten. The history of the circus is dominated by dynasties such as Hagenbeck, the Franconis, the Ringling Brothers and, perhaps the most famous, Barnum and Bailey's Greatest Show on Earth. As in any large family, life in a circus is not always harmonious and tensions are bound to arise from time to time. The story I am about to tell began in one of the smaller establishments.

A typical circus performance in those days consisted of the overture, performing animals, juggling, wire-walking and the flying trapeze. A team of clowns is the icing on the cake, and in our particular story Elsa the female clown was the darling of the audience. Her vivacity and charm had also captivated Arthur, the conductor of the band, who fell passionately in love with her. In this he was not alone, but had to compete with the attentions of Adrian, the trapeze artist.

The highlight of every evening was the flying trapeze act performed by Adrian and his partner Brian. Both had to swing blindfolded without a safety net and exchange trapezes at a certain moment. Arthur selected this act to eliminate his competitor.

How did he do it without in any way interfering with the equipment?

THE ROBBERS

Two robbers break into a jewellery store closed for the weekend and proceed to select the choicest pieces from the display cases. Suddenly one says to the other, "The police are coming, let's take what we have and go." At first the first robber looks mystified as he had neither heard nor seen any evidence that the police were in the vicinity but, turning to the second robber, he looks concerned and says, "OK, let's go."

Explain.

THE CAREFUL DRIVER

I'm driving down a highway at the totally legal 55-miles-per-hour speed limit. I'm sober; my licence plates, licence and insurance are in order and I'm wearing my seat belt. I passed three cars without going over 55 miles per hour, yet a state patrol officer pulled me over and gave me a ticket.

Why?

THE MASK

A man doing a dangerous and difficult job has to wear a mask for protection. Suddenly he tears off his mask and as a consequence he dies. He is not under the influence of drugs or alcohol, and does not intend to commit suicide. So, what makes him tear off his mask?

THE ANTIQUE CANDELABRUM

The scene is a famous antique shop in London's Bond Street. A white Rolls-Royce pulls up and a liveried chauffeur opens the door for an elegant, distinguished-looking elderly man, who enters the antique dealer's. He points at a seventeenth-century candelabrum in the window. He examines it closely, then engages in an animated dialogue with the owner of the shop. Eventually he writes a cheque for £5,000 and departs with the candelabrum.

Shortly thereafter the owner makes a number of telephone calls before closing the shop. Two days later, he receives a call which clearly gets him excited.

In the meantime the distinguished-looking man can be seen in his room at the Ritz, carefully wrapping the candelabrum he bought two days before. He hands it to a younger man, whom he calls Robert. Robert leaves the hotel, hails a taxi and goes to the same antique shop. There, he hands the candelabrum to the owner, who pays him £9,000 in cash.

Explain.

MASS MURDER?

A man who lived alone in a remote part of the country was finally driven insane by his seclusion. One night, during a storm, he switched off the lights, doused the fire, shut all his windows, bolted the front door and set off, never to be seen or heard of again. But by morning, he had caused the deaths of 160 people.

How?

THE ENDURANCE TEST

The Sahara, named after the Arabic word *Sahrá* (wilderness) is the largest desert in the world. When North Africa was still part of the French Empire, members of the Foreign Legion were subjected to a very severe training programme. One of the tests included a forced five-day march through the central Sahara to Fort Flatters with only a loaf of bread and half a litre of water. Several soldiers had to give up halfway and report to the First Aid post located two days away from the starting point. Those who managed the course arrived in a more or less debilitated condition. Hans Mueller, a German who had joined the Legion to escape an unhappy love affair, was the first to arrive at Fort Flatters, tired and sweating profusely but otherwise in surprizingly good physical shape. He expected to be commended for his prowess but instead his colonel told him: "You are not worthy of belonging to the elite of the Foreign Legion and you are discharged."

Why?

THE CAT

The story I am about to tell you formed the background to the 1955 movie *To Catch a Thief* starring Grace Kelly and Cary Grant. It had the usual happy ending but what the scriptwriter did not know was that an innocent man, but for the astute mind of Inspector Chavrol, very nearly became the victim of a miscarriage of justice.

"The Cat" was the name given to a notorious jewel thief who selected as his field of activity the Riviera from Cannes to Monte Carlo. Clearly he had a preference for sunny climates and luxurious ambience. He was a master of disguise and although his methods varied, his favourite modus operandi was to book into an expensive suite in a five-star hotel for a weekend and after a decent interval of time use a duplicate key to help himself to anything he thought was worth having.

Suspicion fell upon a handsome American bachelor who lived in a rented villa in Cap Ferat. His name was Brian Lewis and he spent his days swimming and playing tennis, often in the company of beautiful women. His only link to the robberies was the fact that he had stayed in some of the suites many months before: hardly sufficient evidence to warrant an arrest.

However, one summer evening Betty the chambermaid surprized someone in suite 314/15 rifling the bedroom, and in spite of his beard, she had recognized Brian Lewis, she was certain who had been a guest before. Chavrol was sceptical about the beard, probably false, or if not Brian Lewis would no doubt have shaved it off. Routine enquiries soon confirmed that André, Cannes' most fashionable barber, had indeed relieved a customer answering Brian's description of his whiskers. "Beard or no beard," Chavrol thought, "he is our man." Lewis was brought in for questioning, positively identified by André and Betty, and had no credible alibi. Nevertheless after he had made a statement, Chavrol had to let him go.

What did Brian Lewis point out?

THE BARBER'S SHOP

One day, late afternoon, a man – let's call him David – opens the door to a barber's shop in which only one man, the owner, serves his customers. A man is being shaven, but there are three others waiting. "How long will you be?" asks David. The barber, after a little reflection, replies, "Oh, about an hour." "Thank you," says David and leaves.

About the same time, a few days later, the same scenario occurs except that David's waiting time is reduced to 40 minutes. Again David acknowledges and leaves. The following day the barber is about to finish with a customer and there is no one waiting. "I can take you straight away," says the barber. David is taken aback, but thanks him and leaves the shop.

Explain.

THE EXPERIMENT

Alex was working on an important experiment. Unfortunately, through his carelessness, the experiment was a complete failure. Yet strangely enough, Alex – who was comparatively unknown in his profession – became a world celebrity because of his negligence.

Explain.

SMART KID

I have long been an ardent chess player and my 12-year-old daughter scarcely knows the moves. Recently, two of my chess-expert friends came to dinner. After eating, I played one game with each of them and lost both games.

I had the advantage of a pawn and the opening move. Just as we finished, my daughter came into the room. On learning of my ill success she said: "Daddy, I'm ashamed of you! I can do better than that. Let me play them. I don't want any advantage: I'll play one game with white pieces and one with black. I'll even give them an advantage by playing both games at once and I'll make out better than you did." And she did! How did she do it?

GAME-SET-MATCH

Ernest and Erwin were brothers and very keen on tennis. They were living on a country estate with its own hard tennis court, which they used extensively, trying to improve their game. Unfortunately the court was laid out North to South, so that the player occupying the North end had to face the sun, which made serving very difficult. Although Erwin was a good player, Ernest was only a beginner, and quite often balls had to be recovered from outside the court. To make the game still more difficult, there was usually a strong breeze blowing from the South.

The normal arrangement would have been for the players to change places after each game, but they agreed that it would be in their best interests if Ernest were to play from the North end in spite of the fact that, being the weaker player, he would also suffer the handicap of the sun and the wind. Why?

THE ROLLS-ROYCE CORNICHE

Ronnie Breskal and Ernesto Saler have been friends for many years. Ronnie has reached the pinnacle of his profession, enjoying all the trappings of a successful career – a beautiful house, expensive cars, the lot. Ernesto works in the same industry though much less successfully, at least in terms of financial rewards. Nevertheless Ernesto feels no envy. On the contrary, he admires Ronnie and tries to emulate him in many ways. He often wears similar clothes to Ronnie's and works hard at trying to look like his idol.

One sunny spring morning he takes Ronnie's brand new Rolls-Royce Corniche for a spin. He races along a narrow mountain road and, as he is trying to negotiate a tight bend at excessive speed, loses control and the car catapults into space. Ernesto just manages to jump clear. The Corniche, which was not even insured, becomes a total write-off.

Ronnie, far from being angry, seems slightly amused, congratulates Ernesto and gives it no further thought. Can you explain Ronnie's strange indifference?

LAST LETTER

A woman is seated and is writing. There is a thunderstorm outside and she dies as a consequence. How did she die?

DAILY ROUTINE

Joe leaves his house at 9 a.m. sharp every weekday morning and walks down the block to the corner of a busy street. He stops in front of the general store situated on the corner, then turns and faces the store window with an expectant smile on his face. After a couple of minutes he crosses the road to catch the 9.30 a.m. train to his workplace in the city.

Explain.

SUICIDE

Henry Miller and his wife, Ann, were teaching at the same college. Henry was a philologist and Ann a physicist. They were also joint treasurers and as such, had control of the college's funds. At a recent annual audit it was found that a considerable sum was missing. Henry and Ann were interviewed by the police, then allowed to go home.

The next morning the housekeeper arrived as usual. Finding the door to the bedroom closed and getting no response to her knock, she opened it and discovered their bodies, together with a typed note: "This is the only way out for Ann and I." The police officers were calling it suicide until one of them shook his head in disagreement. What aroused his suspicion?

THE KANGAROO COURT

During the 1950s and 60s a terrorist group active in Germany was trying to destabilize the ruling establishment. One cell, consisting of a young woman and five men, kidnapped a junior official of the Ministry of the Interior. They held a mock trial, accusing him of being responsible for brutal police tactics, and duly sentenced him to death. One of the terrorists, Hans Helldorf, who had particularly suffered police brutality, volunteered to carry out the execution. He quickly shot the official three times at close range, stepping back to avoid the blood as the man pitched forward. Hans then reached down to check the man's pulse, nodded with satisfaction and the group departed hurriedly.

The next morning, terrorist murder made the headlines in all the papers. A few days later Helldorf met a high-ranking police officer in plainclothes and confessed. The policeman made notes, shook hands with Helldorf and departed. Explain.

DRINK-DRIVE

With the festive season approaching, the chief of police ordered a clampdown on drinking and driving. In line with the order, two of his officers were keeping a discreet watch on an exclusive downtown club when they saw a customer stagger out of the door and fall down on the snow-covered ground. After a few seconds he picked himself up, stumbled to his car and fumbled for the keys. Eventually he got the door open and managed to start the car, grinding the gears before moving off in a zigzag course.

The police car followed, stopped him and gave him a breathalyzer test. The test was negative. Obviously something was wrong with the equipment, as the man reeked of alcohol. The officers took him to the police station for another test. Again, negative. A blood test showed the same result. The police were baffled. Can you solve the mystery?

THE TWO SOLICITORS

Smith and Jones are partners in a small firm of solicitors dealing mostly with corporate clients. Jones had worked for a much larger organization but, as he became impatient with the slow pace of promotion, he had made a change. Smith is eight years his junior and is working in the same office as Jones, acting effectively as his assistant.

One morning, just before noon, Jones's secretary bursts into the office, full of excitement: "Mr Jones, the hospital just phoned; your wife has given birth to twins." On hearing this Smith paled, got hold of a paperweight and threw it at Jones.

Explain!

ALL SYSTEMS GO!

Space centres such as Cape Canaveral are usually located in tropical climates. Is there a reason for this?

COPACABANA

Gambling can be as addictive as alcohol or drugs, and Gert Waterman had had his fair share of it. Joining Gamblers Anonymous did the trick and he considered himself cured. His parents were overjoyed, and as a reward gave him a Rolex and offered to pay for a two-week vacation in Rio de Janeiro.

Gert had always wanted to visit Brazil, and the thought of escaping the gloom of a London winter for the sunny beaches of Copacabana filled him with excited anticipation. Unfortunately he had got into bad company during his gambling days and was left in no doubt as to the consequences if he failed to pay the £2,500 he still owed. He could not ask his parents after all they had done for him, and in his desperation he sold the Rolex. Anyway, who needed a watch when there were clocks everywhere? To Gert time was not of the essence anyway. The proceeds just covered his debt.

Arriving in Rio he checked in at the Ouro Verde and spent the days basking in the glorious sunshine of the Copacabana and Ipanema beaches. The one thought which marred his otherwise blissful happiness was how to explain the missing Rolex to his parents.

On the last day of his vacation, fate intervened. He was on the way to his hotel to start packing when he was mugged by a man wielding a knife. Without hesitation, he handed over his money, traveller's cheques and camera and, with some regret, even his signet ring. Although there were many people around, nobody came to his aid and the culprit at once made off with his haul.

On the way to the police station Gert suddenly had an inspiration. This incident could be the *deus ex machina* of all his problems. Police Inspector Nivaldo Garcia typed the report with the list of items, to which Gert added the Rolex watch. He then asked for a copy to support his insurance claim. Nivaldo hesitated for a moment and, looking sternly at Gert, deleted the Rolex from the list of items!

What made the Inspector take this action?

THE MOUNTAIN

Ali lived in a very beautiful little village nestled in a valley in southern Turkey. An avid mountain-climber, every weekend he climbed the nearby mountain. However, although he was a very proficient climber, he always turned back just before he reached the peak. Why?

PLANE CRASH

Alfie Huberman had always been interested in flying, and when he was retired early with a very generous golden handshake he indulged himself by purchasing a new Piper Apache. It had not come cheap, but then nothing does in this life. He couldn't wait to take it up for its maiden flight.

The day was perfect and Alfie was filled with excited anticipation. As expected it flew like a bird, and he looped the loop and swooped low over the field. Suddenly the engine cut out and the plane started to drop like a lead weight. Alfie struggled frantically with the controls, to no avail. His Piper crashed to the ground in an open field and was totally destroyed.

However, other than suffering from shock Alfie was completely unhurt and, surprizingly, although there were other people about, noone took any notice of the accident.

Explain.

STRANGERS ON A TRAIN

A man boarded a train and sat opposite the only other occupant in his carriage, a woman whom he had never met before. As the train started moving, the woman, who did not recognize the man, took a pen and a sheet of paper from her bag and handed them to him. He wrote something on the paper and returned it to her. The woman left the train at the next stop and threw the note away. At no time had they spoken to each other, nor had the meeting been prearranged.

Explain.

TWIN
BROTHER

The publishers of *The Guinness Book of Records* received the following letter:

> *Gentlemen*
>
> *As I am the only registered civil engineer in the state of California who has a twin brother who is also a registered civil engineer in the same state, I believe I deserve a mention in your publication.*
>
> *Yours sincerely*
>
> *Kurt Wilton*

The editor phoned Kurt the next day. 'Surely, Mr. Wilton, you have contradicted yourself in your letter, and therefore you cannot possibly qualify.' Explain.

THE COMPETITORS

Mike and Steve were both senior account executives in different advertizing agencies. Outside business they were close friends, frequently lunching together, comparing notes on the state of the industry, but at the same time being very careful not to divulge any business secrets.

Both companies were successful in acquiring new important instant coffee accounts for TV advertizing. Mike's agency was to handle Brand "X" using an amorous theme, while Steve decided with Brand "Y" to evoke the spirit of adventure, campfire on the prairie, loneliness, with the cup of coffee substituting for a companion. When the two campaigns were in full swing the manufacturers of Brand "X" found to their disappointment that turnover of their brand collapsed, while Brand "Y" increased by 24 per cent.

Subsequently Mike and Steve met for one of their regular lunches. As a consequence of a very serious discussion between the two, during which Mike issued an ultimatum, the turnover in Brand "X" soon recovered thereafter.

Explain.

A JOB IN A MILLION

Robert Bradley is a lucky man indeed. He is only 29 and works for an important corporation with offices all over the world. Robert travels extensively, always first class, staying at the best hotels. He does not buy or sell anything and yet is in close contact with important business people and even royalty. When he speaks, everyone listens with undivided attention.

Arriving at his chosen destination, he spends his time at the swimming pool, if he is not out shopping. After a day or two he leaves, without having concluded any business. Explain.

THE PARIS FAIR

Catherine and her brother, Paul, arrived in Paris from New York the day before the official opening of the World's Fair. They checked in at the Ritz, Paul occupying Room 13 and Catherine one floor higher at Number 25.

Though exhausted from the long trip, they decided to have a light dinner in the grill room before retiring. Halfway through the meal Paul could hardly keep his eyes open, showing extreme fatigue, so he decided to go to his room, leaving Catherine to finish her dessert.

It was almost noon the next day before Catherine woke up. She dressed in a hurry as she had arranged to attend the fair's opening ceremony with Paul at 1 p.m. When she was ready she asked the operator to connect her to Room 13. There was a moment's silence; then the operator replied, "But Madame, there is no Room 13 in this hotel." Catherine frowned. Had she mistaken the room number?

She went down to the concierge and asked again for Room 13, but got the same reply: "You know, Madame, superstition and all that." "Well, what room is my brother in?" "Your brother? But Madame arrived alone last evening." The concierge produced the hotel register, which showed Catherine's entry but nothing about Paul. By this time Catherine had become frantic and called for the manager. Together with him, she went to the first floor. Indeed, there were Rooms 12 and 14, but no 13.

This is supposed to be a true story. Can you figure out what was happening?

MARITAL PROBLEM

Jason and Dean were brothers. Jason married Jackie, and Dean married Denise. However, Jason and Denise have the same wedding anniversary. Dean's wedding anniversary was one month before this date and Jackie's was one month after it. There have been no divorces or remarriages.

How do you explain this?

POLAR EXPEDITION

A German team led by Von Hasseldorf and a British team under Sir Tony Priday were racing toward the North Pole.

The British base kept in close radio contact with their team and reports were broadcast around the world to follow the progress of both teams. On one occasion the following dialogue developed:

Base: What is your position and how is the team coping?

Sir Henry: We have just passed the point which Nansen reached in April 1895. Our team is in good health and spirits, although Brian is suffering from frostbite.

Base: What is the weather like?

Sir Henry: The snowstorm has abated and it is now clear and sunny. The temperature is minus 40 degrees.

Base: Is that Celsius or Fahrenheit?

Sir Henry: It is... (crackle, crackle).

The connection was then broken and could not be restored. Nevertheless the correct temperature was recorded and transmitted to the media. How could this be possible?

38

UPSIDE DOWN

A man is observed by several onlookers to walk slowly and hesitantly from one corner of a large room to the opposite side. He describes what he sees, which is everything turned upside down. He walks normally, wears neither spectacles nor contact lenses, is not suffering from a disease and his eyes are perfectly in order.

Can you find an explanation for this strange behaviour?

POLICE EMERGENCY

The police had been called to a farmhouse 20 miles outside town where they arrested a particularly vicious psychopath, who had previously murdered two of the farm's occupants. They were returning to the police station when the prisoner attacked the officer sitting with him in the back of the police car. The driver immediately called his station and asked for urgent backup.

The station had only one other car in the vicinity and called it on the radio. However, the officers did not respond and, as a result, both officers escorting the prisoner were killed and the prisoner escaped. The officers in the second police car were amazed when, upon returning to the station, they were charged with dereliction of duty. Their radio was in perfect working order and yet they had not responded to the emergency call.

Why not?

WHAT AM I?

If you look, you can't see me.
If you see me, you cannot see anything else.
I can make you walk if you cannot.
Sometimes I speak the truth.
And sometimes I lie.
If I lie, I am nearer the truth.

What am I?

ROUGE ET NOIR

The scene: A famous Monte Carlo casino. A distinguished gentleman with a stunning brunette at his side is playing red or black at the roulette table. Watching them is another couple nearby.

George Benson and Isabelle Labrue start to talk. "You know, Isabelle, I often wonder why Philip Castle continues to play. He loses most of the time – roughly 500,000 francs a year." "He must be very rich," Isabelle offers. "Not really," responds George. "His wife, Deborah, the lovely creature by his side, is the one with the money and she finances him." "She must be very much in love or very stupid, or she would leave him and find someone with better luck." "On the contrary, she is quite happy with the situation," says George, with a knowing smile.

Why?

THE MOTOR POOL

Otto Fischer is chief executive of Sunlight Limited, a company in the leisure industry. Sunlight has a fleet of 10 cars, all of the same make and in almost constant use. Their average mileage is about 2,000 per annum. They are in very good condition and hardly ever break down. Altogether a very smooth operation, with only one unusual feature: some tyres on all cars – and always the same – suffer greater wear than others.

Why should this be so?

BANK ROBBERY

The district bank's branch in Coleridge occupied a quaint corner building in the main street. The manager, Richard West, controlled a staff of five. Sets of keys to the premises were kept by the manager, his assistant and the cleaner.

On the Friday before Christmas, the local traders deposited their week's receipts with the bank, where the money was kept in a somewhat antiquated safe in the manager's office. The safe needed two keys to open it one held by the manager and one by his assistant.

The bank boasted a primitive burglar alarm which allowed 30 seconds after opening the premises for the alarm to be switched off. For additional protection, a guard was employed to walk around the corner block, which took 10 minutes. Whenever the guard passed the manager's office he could satisfy himself, by looking through a peephole, that the door of the safe remained intact.

The following Monday morning, the cleaner entered the premises and saw immediately that the safe had been broken into using an acetylene torch. The police were puzzled as the guard assured them that he had walked his rounds as usual and had seen the safe intact until going off duty, just before the cleaner arrived. On the other hand, to crack the safe was a good hour's work.

Explain.

EXHIBIT "A"

The atmosphere in the court room was tense. The prosecutor was uneasy as he felt that the jury was not entirely on his side. True, the alibi of the accused, Henry Thompson, was flimsy. But on the other hand how many of us can remember what we were doing two months ago between 3 and 4 p.m? The murder weapon – a knife, admitted as Exhibit A – belonged to the accused but he claimed to have lost it long before. Or had it perhaps been stolen? One vital piece of evidence which could clinch the case was missing: the murder was committed by a right-handed criminal, while the defendant claimed he was left-handed although in fact he was ambidextrous.

In his desperation the prosecutor recalled the defendant. Raising the murder weapon and addressing the jury he said, with an undertone of drama: "This, ladies and gentlemen, is by his own admission the property of the accused and the only fingerprints found on the weapon are his." At this moment when everyone's attention was focused on the knife, he turned toward the defendant, shouting, "Catch!" and threw the murder weapon at him. By instinctively catching the knife, Henry Thompson provided the vital missing link and was found guilty by the jury.

Explain the missing link.

THE ODD SOCK

It happened at Charles de Gaulle Airport in Paris. Passengers arriving by Concorde from Rio de Janeiro were waiting for their luggage at conveyor number 3. Suddenly a gaily coloured solitary sock, obviously fallen out of a suitcase, was travelling around the conveyor belt. Passengers looked at each other with amusement until a remark made by one of them sent the crowd roaring with laughter.

What was the remark?

There are probably a number of different comments which would have a similar effect, but the reader is expected to find, by clever questioning, this book's solution, which is considered to be the funniest.

SECRETS OF THE LAKE

Until she decided to take her husband's tuxedo to the cleaners, Madeleine was at peace with the world. She had it all: a beautiful house bordering Lake Léman, near Geneva, and a handsome husband, Rene, who had an executive position with Banque Romande on a substantial salary. Madeleine herself was a partner in the law firm of Dkverin-Millefleurs in Lausanne. The couple had two lovely children – twins, a boy and a girl, 10 years old. But when Madeleine emptied the pockets of the tuxedo, she found a torrid love letter written by her best friend, Desirée. Her world collapsed and for days she struggled with the torture of the knowledge and whether or not she should confront Rene.

One late afternoon she took the children on a motorboat ride on the lake. Two hours later she returned alone, completely distraught and in a state of severe shock. Questioned by the police, she told the story of a catastrophic outing. The children had tried to retrieve something they had seen floating in the lake and had fallen overboard. Madeleine had been unable to save them.

The story made little sense to the police, particularly as Madeleine was known to be a good swimmer. Also, since her clothes were dry, she had obviously not made a serious attempt to rescue the twins. The terrible suspicion hardened when, on searching the house, the police found Desirée's letter.

After several hours of intensive interrogation, Madeleine couldn't hold out any longer and made a full confession. However, after studying the case, the Juge d'Instruction decided not to proceed and Madeleine was released without charge. Explain.

THE FATAL BULLET

Mario Franchesci was deeply troubled. He was infatuated with his girlfriend Sylvia and could not accept the thought that she would have to die. There was proof that Sylvia had broken the strict law of Omerta, never to betray the Cosa Nostra – she had been observed entering the DA's office in disguise. The conclusion was clear. The Capo di Tutti Capi had instructed Mario to eliminate her. Mario had resisted, and as a consequence his own position was in jeopardy.

As he paced up and down in his study, chain-smoking, he knew in his heart of hearts that he would have to do the deed. He walked two blocks to Sylvia's apartment and opened the door with his own key. He tip toed into her bedroom. Sylvia was asleep. Mario looked at her with a mixture of love and anguish. He held the gun close to her temple and pulled the trigger. It felt as if he had shot himself.

Two days later he was arrested. Mario had been careless. The gun was still in his possession and forensics had no difficulty in establishing that the bullet had come from it. Surprizingly, however, Mario was released the same afternoon, all charges against him having been dropped.

Explain.

THE CHAPEL

Henry Morgan was not a deeply religious man. However, he preferred to play safe and in a crisis he invariably took to prayer. He reasoned that if there was someone who listened, it just might help; if not, no harm was done.

Once again one of his property deals had gone wrong and Henry was in serious trouble. The only thing that could save him from bankruptcy was *force majeure*, an Act of God, such as an earthquake or at least subsidence, as he was heavily insured. For a brief moment he had considered lending a helping hand toward such an event, but the advanced state of forensic science scared him off.

He therefore made his way to his favourite chapel on Mont St. Michel. It was a good hour's walk in the glaring midday sun. On arrival he first sat down to rest his tired legs. When he had finished his prayers a couple of hours later, he found to his exasperation that he was unable to walk back home. He was not incapacitated in any way, nor had anything unusual occurred in the landscape.

Can you explain what had happened?

SALE OF THE YEAR

Berner's department store in North Finchley held their annual sale, which was considered a social event in all the surrounding districts. Prices were marked down by as much as 50 per cent and for some items as much as 70 per cent.

Queues were forming by 5 a.m. for opening at 9 a.m. By that time the line stretched almost around the whole block. Just before opening time a man arrived by taxi and immediately pushed himself to the front of the queue. Angry shouts sent him back toward the end of the line-up. He did not utter a word and his pleading look was to no avail. He tried again, but angry voices and veiled threats forced him to retreat. On his third attempt he was physically attacked and pushed from the pavement.

After he recovered his composure, he took a piece of paper from his pocket and wrote a few lines, which he showed to the people next to him. Whatever he wrote spread like wildfire throughout the queue, resulting in a great deal of amusement and some embarrassment.

What do you think the note said?

THE DAGGER

Following an emergency call Detective Inspector Miller, accompanied by his assistant Norman, entered one of the Georgian-style houses in exclusive Bishops Avenue. The housekeeper, in a state of shock, guided Miller into the study, where he saw the art collector Professor Maynard slumped over his desk. He had been killed with a dagger from his own collection, a fifteenth-century broad-bladed Cinquedeas weapon.

Maynard's nephew Albert, who had discovered the body, reported: "At about 10 a.m. I knocked on my uncle's study door and as there was no response, I opened the door and found what you see now. I did not touch anything, but at once phoned 999, and that is all I know." Just then the forensic team arrived and did their work. Miller noticed that the french door to the garden was slightly open.

The lab report established the time of death as between 9 and 10 a.m. and no fingerprints were found on the dagger. The killer had obviously worn gloves. Miller pondered the report for a while. Suddenly he had a flash of inspiration. He asked Norman to apply for a warrant to arrest Albert for the murder of his uncle.

What proof did Miller have?

THE CAR CRASH

Jim Jones was driving home in his car, with his son, Robert, in the passenger seat. The car was involved in a crash with a lorry, and Jim was killed outright. Robert was seriously injured and taken to hospital in an ambulance. In the operating theatre, the surgeon looked at Robert and said, "I'm sorry, but I can't operate on this patient – he is my son, Robert."

What is the explanation?

PERIL IN THE SKY

When I drove Richard to the Sport Parachute Club at Elstree, little did I know that I would be witness to an amazing event more bizarre than any fiction writer's imagination could devize. But let me tell you the whole story.

It was a brilliant summer's day, not a cloud in the sky, ideal for the multiple formation sky-diving which was on the club's programme for that sunny afternoon. Driving down the country lane leading to the clubhouse in an open MG convertible with a balmy breeze in my hair was an exhilarating experience.

At the club, preparations for the day's diving agenda were in full swing. As the aged Dakota was about to start the motors and the first 20 divers approached the aircraft, Richard had to hurry to don his nylon jump-suit and assemble his gear. He was the last to board the Dakota and snap into the static line.

The plan was to jump at 10,000 feet before pulling the ripcord. A parachute pack contains two parachutes as a safety measure, and it is considered inconceivable that both would fail. Richard, being last on the static line, was the last to jump. And then it happened: Richard did not join the others, but lagged behind. Obviously something was terribly wrong. To make matters worse, both his parachutes failed to open.

Miraculously he survived with minor injuries. The strangest thing of all was this: had the parachute opened, Richard would probably be dead. What do you make of this bizarre story, which happens to be true?

THE CADILLAC

Three men from the drug enforcement department of HM Customs were waiting at Southampton Docks for the arrival of the Queen Elizabeth from New York.

As the first-class passengers disembarked, the Customs men were watching unobtrusively those passengers who were waiting for their cars to be unloaded. A black Cadillac was one of the first. When they could read the registration number, the three Customs officers looked at each other with a faint smile of recognition.

The Cadillac sped toward London, followed by Customs cars, changing at regular intervals like a relay to avoid detection. When the Cadillac drove into a garage near Heston, the pursuers pounced. They knew exactly where to look and dismantled the door panels from which they retrieved 20 bags of white powder weighing one kilogramme each. The four occupants of the Cadillac were arrested.

When the lab report eventually came through it caused a mild sensation: the plastic bags were found to contain ordinary flour. What were the occupants trying to do, assuming their purpose was not to divert attention?

SPRING IN THE MOUNTAINS

During a vacation, a hiker discovered the bodies of a middle-aged couple holding hands in a remote field near the Austrian village of St. Anton. Suicide was ruled out, there was no visible evidence of cause of death that would indicate murder, nor was any poison found on medical examination. How did the couple die?

55

THE SHOPPING MALL

Herbert Tidy, an efficiency expert, and his wife, Harriet, decided to visit the new shopping mall which had just opened in town. There, Harriet became so involved with the items on display in a hat shop that she didn't notice her husband wasn't with her. When she discovered he wasn't around, her first reaction was to go and look for him; then she remembered what he was always telling her: If two people are trying to find each other, it is more efficient if one stands still than if both search. She was quite happy with this theory as it gave her time to look at more hats until her husband arrived. Despite her recollection of her husband's theory on the efficiency of searches, the strategy was unwise. Suggest why.

THE SLOW HORSES

Alexander, the aged and eccentric king of Draconia, decided to abdicate but could not make up his mind which of his two sons should sit on his throne. He finally decided that, as his sons were both accomplished horsemen, he would hold a race in which the loser, i.e. the owner of the slowest, rather than the fastest horse, would become king.

Each of the sons owned a superb horse and feared that the other would cheat by holding his own horse back, so they agreed to consult the wisest man in the kingdom. With only two words, the wise man ensured that the race would be fair. What did he say?

PILOT ERROR

Tim Shaw, a pilot for 18 years, had an outstanding safety record. One afternoon he was trying to land a British Airways 747. Visibility was good in spite of a slight snow flurry. He was easing the plane gently down toward the runway when it happened. It appeared that Tim had throttled back too early and the Jumbo jet, one of the safest planes in service, stalled and crash-landed.

Although no one was hurt, the accident was clearly due to pilot error, yet Tim was not grounded. He continued flying and, in spite of this blemish on his record, his career remained unaffected. How was this possible, considering the stringent safety measures applied by all international airlines?

THE VENTURE

Two men decided to embark on a venture which promised to be extremely rewarding financially. They pooled their resources to buy the equipment they needed and after some extensive promotion, they got underway. Unfortunately, in due course they had to discard some of the material they had bought, in order to save their lives.

What were they up to?

PRESUMPTION OF AUTHORITY

Lee Dawson was 15 minutes early for his appointment with Stuart Gaylord, junior partner in Mitchell, Rosenbloom, O'Leary, Saffran & Loeb. He was requested to await the appointed time although he could observe through the glass partition that Gaylord was sitting at his desk doing nothing except puffing a cigar.

At 3 p.m. sharp, Dawson was ushered into the panelled office, where Gaylord greeted him with a limp handshake without rising. Offering his client a cigar, he rocked back in his chair, balancing perilously and giving the impression that at any moment he could fall either way. More of a circus act than a legal consultation, Lee thought with some irritation. "What can I do for you, Mr Dawson?" asked Gaylord condescendingly, prepared to dispense jurisprudential wisdom.

Lee Dawson's problem had started with the sale of his stamp collection, but Gaylord let him tell the story in his own words: "I did not know the buyer and therefore I insisted on cash in the amount of $42,000. The same morning I made my way to the Madison Avenue branch of my bank to deposit the funds to the credit of my account. This branch, like most, is organized on the open-plan basis. Having filled in the deposit slip, I approached one of the desks, occupied apparently by George Appleby, vice-president. At this bank everybody but the doorman is a vice-president. Appleby counted the money,

initialled the slip and I departed. When I received the statement
of my account in due course, there was no $42,000 credit. I
visited the bank, produced the paying-in slip to the branch
manager, who pointed out that it was not stamped and that the
initials were not recognized. After further enquiries, it transpired
that Vice-President Appleby had been out for lunch at the time
in question and probably a tired customer had sat down at his
desk for a brief rest. One of Appleby's colleagues was able to
give a description of the stranger to the police, but the bank
denies liability. What do I do now?"

Gaylord, still in balancing mode, decided to play it safe and
adopted a normal sitting position. "You have nothing to worry
about, Mr Dawson. There was a test case a few years ago and

the court decided that the doctrine of presumed authority applies. You had every right to assume that the person sitting at that desk was acting for the bank and therefore the bank is undoubtedly liable. They might still go to court as a matter of principle in the hope of upsetting the previous judgement, but they don't have a chance. If you decide to proceed, we shall be happy to act for you."

During the court hearing 14 months later, the judge upheld the presumption of authority doctrine. Nevertheless because of the statement of one witness, he found for the defence and the case was dismissed.

Can you guess what the witness testified?

MERCADO INC.

Conrad Holt's duties as finance director of Mercado Inc., the international oil traders, included regular tours of inspection of the company's overseas subsidiaries. Dealing in crude oil was a very speculative business and overseas managers had to be strictly controlled. Harry Green, chief executive and major shareholder, had authorized some deals which had gone wrong, resulting in heavy losses. He was therefore particularly concerned to avoid further exposures.

Green instructed Holt to fly to Beirut to examine the books of their wholly-owned subsidiary. In accordance with standard practice in dangerous areas, Mercado took out a substantial insurance policy to cover kidnapping and ransom demands. The premium, although quite high in view of Lebanon's history, was at least tax-deductible. This soon proved to be a very wise precaution, as two days after his arrival Holt was abducted. There was silence for a whole week before the first ransom demand of $3 million arrived from a man who identified himself as a member of Hezbollah. In close cooperation with the insurers, the ransom was negotiated down to $2 million. This was paid as instructed, and Holt was duly released.

A short time after his return to New York in a blaze of publicity, Holt resigned his job and moved to the South of France. He was not to enjoy his luxurious lifestyle for long. The same year he suffered a fatal car accident. On hearing of Holt's death, Harry Green took the first plane to the South of France and broke into Holt's villa.

Explain this strange behaviour.

BUREAU DE CHANGE

If you had followed Tim Copeland on his rounds during the last three days you would hardly have believed your eyes. On Tuesday, after shopping in the supermarket, he went to the High Street bank opposite and bought 1,000 Deutschmarks, although he had no intention of travelling to Germany. On Wednesday, he went to the same bank first thing in the morning and, at a different counter, sold the Deutschmarks against sterling. On Thursday, he went to the hairdresser to shave off his beard, afterwards again to the bank to buy 2,000 Swiss francs. He had never been to Switzerland and did not intend to go there.

What was Tim after?

EAT AND YOU DIE

A woman gave a man something to eat. The food was perfectly edible, nor did the man choke. However, as a consequence of tasting it, he died at a later date.

Explain.

THE JUDGEMENT

A man is tried for the crime of murder and found guilty. The judge says, "This is the strangest case I have ever seen. By all the evidence you are guilty beyond any reasonable doubt, yet the law requires that I set you free."

What is the reason for the judge's decision?

DEAL OF THE YEAR

Frank Forrester's weekend treat was to read all sections of the *Sunday Times* in bed from the first line to the last, including the advertizements. When he came to the classified ads section he noticed something which struck him like a bolt from the blue.

He went to a dealer and, after much haggling, bought something for £1,600. The next day he visited his friend Bruce Miller, who had made his millions in the rag trade, and offered him the same item for £35,000. Bruce did not hesitate, paid cash and had the look of a man who had just secured the bargain of his life. A week later he gave it to his wife as a birthday present and she seemed thrilled beyond words.

Sadly, she had a fatal accident in her Rolls-Royce Corniche shortly thereafter. Bruce had the car repaired and, in the circumstances, was only too anxious to get rid of it. As the car was 12 years old, he got only £30,000 – more or less the market price – but strangely enough, this included the birthday present to his wife.

What do you make of it?

LOADED GUN

The prosecuting counsel stepped forward and faced the jury. "We are supposed to believe that the defendant, although in possession of a loaded gun at the time of the murder, did not commit the crime – indeed, never even took the weapon out of his pocket." The prosecutor looked across at the defendant with a smug smile on his face. "Yes, the defendant stated at the time of his arrest that the gun had remained, unfired, in the right-hand outside pocket of his overcoat, while an unidentified assailant killed the victim. How is it, then, that when the defendant was searched by the police at the time of the arrest, the gun was found in the inside, left-hand pocket of his overcoat?" (The gun was fully loaded when found, but a cartridge could have been replaced after firing and cleaning the gun.)

As he finished speaking, the prosecutor caught a fleeting look of triumph on the defence counsel's face and felt distinctly uneasy. So he should; the defence produced a completely logical explanation for the movement of the gun, although the defendant had not touched it. He was later acquitted.

Explain.

RESEMBLANCE

When Peter flew into Heathrow from New York after a 10-year absence, who should he meet at the airport but an old friend from his grammar school days. They hadn't changed much and would have recognized each other instantly anywhere.

"How have you been keeping and what have you been doing all these years?" Peter asked. "I am fine, thank you. As you will remember, I was always interested in jurisprudence and am now a QC. I also got married to someone from the French Lycée you might have heard of, but never met. Incidentally this girl at my side is my daughter, Lucy." Peter looked at Lucy with a loving smile and said, "Young lady, you look exactly like your mother."

How did he know?

THE PROFESSOR

A true story?

Professor Gauss was Professor of Mathematics at Gottingen University in 1807. Shortly after his appointment, Gauss decided to move to a larger house in the suburbs to accommodate his growing family.

Not wanting to be involved with the chore of moving, he asked his wife to make the necessary arrangements so that he could join the family at the new address after finishing his lectures. By then, while remembering the name of the suburb, he had forgotten the address. He wandered about the neighbourhood, trying to find his bearings.

In the end he approached a policeman: "Excuse me, officer, do you know where the Gauss family lives?" The policeman (recognizing him) replied, "Sorry, Professor Gauss, I really don't know, but why don't you ask the postman over there?" Gauss did, with the same negative response. He then approached a little girl across the street. "Excuse me, little lady, do you happen to know where the Gauss family lives?" The girl's reply sent Gauss into fits of laughter.

Why?

STRANGE BEHAVIOUR

If you could follow Gerald Watson in his tracks you would be intrigued by his irrational behaviour. On 1 December he arrived in Miami and registered at the Doral Hotel in Miami Beach, as he had done for several years. Being a generous tipper, he was well known and liked by the hotel staff.

After a few days he took an early flight to La Guardia. Watson did not leave the airport but stayed in the transit lounge, where he was joined by a beautiful blonde. An hour later, the couple boarded a plane for Miami. At the airport they were met by a limousine from the Hyatt Hotel, Bal Harbour, where they booked a large suite overlooking the sea. Watson returned to the Doral, and for the following few days went back and forth between the two hotels, having two breakfasts and spending alternate nights in each.

What was Gerald Watson up to?

THE UNFAITHFUL WIFE

John, an author, had suspected for some time that his wife Eva was unfaithful, though he had no proof.

One afternoon, as John was working on his latest novel, Eva mentioned that she intended to go to the cinema and would be out for a few hours. As Eva went to the door, John looked at her pensively and then returned
to his work.

Three hours later Eva returned, took her coat off and asked John whether he wanted some coffee. When she returned from the kitchen, John asked her to sit down as he wanted to talk to her.

"Eva" he said, "I want a divorce."

Why?

WOLF AMONG THE SHEEP

An old wolf had spent days crossing a vast wasteland without anything to eat. Starving, he came upon a large metal enclosure in the middle of a field. Inside the compound were many very fat, well-fed sheep. The walls of the enclosure were so high and the bars so close together that it was impossible for the sheep or anything to escape once inside. Due to his long fast, however, the wolf was so thin that he knew he could squeeze in through the bars and feast himself on the sheep to his heart's content. Although hunger urged him on, the wily wolf also realized that, after he ate his fill, he would be unable to escape. The wolf sat and pondered and then found an ingenious solution.
What did the wolf do?

THE BESTSELLER

Victor Bronson, the author, had invited a select circle of friends to a dinner party, to be followed by a reading from his latest novel, which had been on the bestseller list for the last two months. After an excellent meal, coffee was served and the guests settled down comfortably to listen to the reading of *Moon Harvest.* As the story unfolded even his friends who had not read the book were enchanted by the style and depth of the masterful writing. Fred Gordon, his publisher, recorded the reading with a view to producing a CD edition.

Suddenly all the lights went out, and it was soon discovered that the blackout had affected the whole neighbourhood. Yet, although no flashlights or candles were available, Victor continued reading without hesitation; and when the tape was later compared with the book it was found that the recording was identical, word for word, with the text.

Did Victor simply have a phenomenal memory?

THE MAGNA CARTA

The Empire Museum had recently been in the news a great deal. The media devoted whole columns to the installation of the latest state-of-the-art security systems. After all, the museum housed a vast collection of items famous for their richness and variety. The most outstanding objects were one of the four surviving copies of King John's Magna Carta (1215) and the original score of Handel's Messiah. Each of these two pieces was of inestimable value.

The centrepiece of the new system was the introduction of electronic sensors below the floors, which were so sensitive that small adjustments were necessary when a passing lorry, and on another occasion a mouse, set off the alarm. Needless to say, access to the skylight was also made impossible as the parapet surrounding the roof was wired.

It was perhaps an innate trait of Eric Wilton's personality that he considered the extravagant claims of impregnable security an irresistible challenge. Eric planned carefully. He enlisted the help of an adventurous friend who owned a helicopter. A foggy November night seemed ideal timing. With the helicopter hovering, Eric abseiled, cut the skylight, and removed the pane. He then lowered himself head-first, just above the showcase protecting the Magna Carta. At that moment, disaster struck. A packet of cigarettes fell from his pocket to the floor and all hell broke loose. His friend escaped, but Eric Wilton was arrested and promptly charged.

Strangely enough, an unrelated event on the morning of his arrest decisively affected Eric's life. A motor car travelling east on the M4 collided with a bus and burst into flames, killing John Reynolds, the driver.

In due course, Eric was jailed for eight years. It seems bizarre, but had the M4 accident not happened, Eric would have only been fined or sentenced to three months' community service. Incidentally he did not know Reynolds, had never met him or spoken to him.

Explain.

DEAL A BRIDGE HAND

Andrew Abelson had dealt about half of the cards for a bridge game when he was interrupted by a telephone call. When he returned to the table, no one could remember where he had dealt the last card. Without counting the number of cards in any of the four partly-dealt hands, or the number of cards yet to be dealt, how could he continue to deal accurately, with everyone getting exactly the same cards he would have had if the deal had not been interrupted?

ENIGMATIC DIALOGUE

A stranger pushed his way into the bank as Tom the guard was about to close. He wore a balaclava and carried a Sainsbury's carrier bag. He pushed a piece of paper across the counter and mumbled, "No fifties."

Tom was on his guard, and as he approached the counter he heard the stranger making conversation with Elsa. Tom withdrew hastily, but even after the man had left unhurriedly, the police were not called. However, the bank later informed the police and lodged a claim with the insurance company in due course.

Explain.

WITNESSES FOR THE DEFENCE

Bruce and Harry had planned the bank hold-up with the greatest of care. The victim was a suburban branch of the First State Bank on a Friday afternoon, one minute before closing. All the cash from the local shops would be there for the weekend, and if the robbers locked the doors behind them as they entered the bank, no one would be surprized.

The raid went precisely as planned. There was no resistance from the staff, the automatics saw to that – and the haul exceeded their expectations. After the staff was bound and gagged, the robbers left the premises unhurriedly. The video cameras, however, had done their work well, and the police had no problem identifying the culprits, who had worn no disguises, within hours. They were caught the next day.

Although Bruce and Harry strenuously denied being the robbers, every one of the bank's staff identified them, picking them out of police line-ups, so it looked like an open-and-shut case. The prosecution relied on the video films and the testimony of the bank's staff. The defence called only two witnesses, but as a result the judge had to direct the jury to find the defendants not guilty. How do you explain this extraordinary turn of events?

THE ORDINANCE

They called him "Crazy Harry" because of his outlandish ideas on welfare for the community. That is until he was voted – by a majority of three – Mayor of Ulm, a small German town straddling the Danube.

The only licensed barber had little difficulty in persuading Mayor Harry Morgan to pass an ordinance to the effect that no man in Ulm should have a beard, or shave himself, and that only the authorized town barber could shave anyone. The barber, being a resident of Ulm, was however bound by the same law. Yet the ordinance was strictly observed by all Ulmers.

How was this possible?

IRA JUSTICE

In Northern Ireland the IRA have a punishment they mete out to petty criminals or informers known as "knee-capping" (firing a single shot into each kneecap).

One night three IRA members entered a "safe" pub where a man was sitting having a drink. They picked him up and frog-marched him out of the pub and into an adjoining field. Without a word being spoken by the IRA members, they shot the man through both knees. As the shots hit, the man screamed loudly and he fell to the ground. Unmoved by the screams of agony, the men turned around, walked quickly back to their car and sped away.

As the car disappeared into the distance, the man's screams stopped. He got up and walked away.

Explain.

ROBBERY SUSPECT

Detective Steve Roberts was having a tough time with James Nicholson, a suspect who had been arrested in connection with a vicious armed robbery which had taken place at a Baton Rouge bank. He knew that Nicholson had committed the crime along with two other men, but Nicholson had an alibi corroborated by three witnesses. Nicholson claimed he had attended the funeral of an old friend in New Orleans on the day of the robbery and had stuck firmly to his story.

"Why did you attend this funeral?" asked Steve. "Because the deceased had been my best friend at high school," retorted Nicholson. "How was he interred?" pressed Steve. "By burial, of course," sneered Nicholson.

Steve glared at Nicholson with a faint trace of a smile on his face. "You can bribe your crooked friends to lie on your behalf but you have proved that you are not really as clever as you think, Nicholson. I arrest you for armed robbery."

How did Steve Roberts know that Nicholson was lying?

NUISANCE CALLS

Ever since Joan had her photograph published in a Sunday newspaper she was subjected to heavy-breathing telephone calls. In the beginning she just replaced the receiver, hoping that the nuisance caller would tire of wasting time and money.

But the calls kept coming. Then she changed tactics and became abusive. The caller seemed to enjoy her reaction as the calls grew more frequent. In her desperation she contacted her telephone company and the police. They advized her to go ex-directory. In a final attempt to avoid this inconvenience the police suggested that she should try to keep the line open for about one minute, which would be sufficient to trace the calls.

She succeeded by pretending to be interested, and the call was traced to a public coin-operated booth in Paddington. The police pounced and arrested a man who was about to leave the booth. He denied having made any calls as he discovered that he had no change. The police then dusted the receiver for fingerprints as the man watched proceedings with disdain. "I can save you the trouble. You will find my fingerprints as I tried to make a reverse-charge call, but I got tired of waiting for the operator to respond. The man you want probably left the booth about two minutes before you arrived." A body search confirmed that the man had no coins.

Were the police outwitted?

DOUBLE HOMICIDE

A man discovered that his wife had a lover and there was evidence that they intended to kill him. He decided to pre-empt their plan and when, upon returning from a trip, he found them together he killed them both. Realizing that he would be a prime suspect, he had to devize a way to mislead the police. Simply wiping his fingerprints from the murder weapon, a knife, would not help. He managed to produce prints on the knife which would never be traced. How did he do it?

THE PRESIDENTS

Bob glanced up from his newspaper, "Here's an unusual story, Tom. It says here that three of the first five presidents of the United States died on July 4th. I wonder what the odds are against a coincidence like that." "I'm not sure," replied Tom, "but I am willing to give ten-to-one odds that I can name one of the three who died on that date."

Assuming that Tom had no prior knowledge of the dates on which any of the presidents died, was he justified in offering such generous odds?

THE PHONE-IN

Tom Bradley had left his home in Alperton early that day to drive to Manchester for a seminar, spread over three days.

As he drove, he switched on the radio and listened to a phone-in program. The moderator was telephoning London subscribers at random to obtain their views on the performance of public transport in the Greater London area. Tom listened to three opinions with slight amusement, nodding in approval when he agreed with a response. Suddenly his face turned angry. He headed toward the next exit and sped for home.

Explain.

THE SHARPSHOOTER

A sharpshooter hung up his hat and put on a blindfold. He then walked 100 yards, turned around and shot a bullet through his hat. The blindfold was a perfectly good one and completely blocked the man's vision.

How did he manage this feat?

THE X-RAY FILM

Robert Blocker, approaching his fortieth birthday, had never been abroad. He enjoyed his vacations in Torquay and being in charge of UK marketing, he never had a need to travel. All this was to change when he was promoted to the position of export manager for the South American market. He was delighted with the opportunity to visit all these exotic countries. Strangely, though, on every trip he took with him an x-ray film made about 10 years before.

Considering that Blocker was in perfect health and had no intention of consulting a doctor, and his company was in the textile business, how do you account for this unusual habit?

THE EXHUMATION

When Mrs Watson returned home from hospital she could not walk very well but was happy to be on the road to recovery. Two days later she complained of dizziness, but Dr Thompson, who attended her, found nothing wrong.

The following Saturday evening her housekeeper, Helen, noticed a change for the worse. Mrs Watson died at 9 a.m. on the Sunday. Only her husband and Helen were present. Dr Thompson signed the death certificate, giving gastritis as the main cause of death with a heart condition as a contributory factor.

Burial arrangements were made with Geoffrey Griffiths, the local undertaker. The oak coffin was made in his workshop and he himself lifted Mrs Watson's body into the coffin and closed it. When it was carried out, one of the pall-bearers remarked on the size on the coffin and Griffiths explained that the inside was lined with wadding.

The horrifying idea that Mrs Watson's death might not be what it appeared came to Dr Thompson when he happened to study a book on toxicology. The symptoms he had seen resembled those of arsenic poisoning. He contacted Chief Inspector Hill, who in turn applied to the North Hertfordshire coroner for an exhumation order, which was granted at once.

Digging began the following day at noon. The coffin was lifted but the opening postponed to await the arrival of the Chief Inspector and officials from the Home Office. At 3 p.m. the lid was unscrewed to expose a sight which those present will not forget as long as they live. In addition to Mrs Watson, the coffin contained the body of a middle-aged man.

Can you find a rational explanation?

P.S. Incidentally, the suspicion of murder of Mrs Watson by arsenic poisoning proved to be unfounded, though traces of arsenic were found in the dead man.

BABY-MINDER

Susan Carpenter was in a hurry. She had an audition at 10 a.m. and it was already 9.45 a.m. As she passed a drugstore she was stopped by a young woman with a pram. "Would you mind keeping an eye on my baby while I buy some diapers?" she pleaded. Susan looked at her watch and replied, "I really am in a hurry." "It will only take a minute and I will be right back," responded the young woman. Susan reluctantly agreed.

As the minutes ticked by Susan became increasingly restive, especially when the baby started to cry very loudly. Passers-by began to look accusingly at her, which made her even more nervous. In desperation, Susan picked up the baby hoping that it would stop crying. She was utterly amazed to find that the baby was in fact a dummy and that the crying emanated from a tape recorder hidden inside the pram.

What was going on?

OVERHEARD

"I eat what I can, and I can what I can't."

What does that mean?

JILTED BRIDE

In a mountain village in Switzerland a couple were being married. During the ceremony, a girl – jilted by her bridegroom – appeared and made a scene. "The wedding bell will not ring," she said, and immediately took poison and was rushed to hospital.

Sure enough when the bell-ringer tried, there was no sound from the bell. Some said she was a witch and had cast a spell, but others thought she had tied the clapper. After the ceremony they went to the belfry but found everything in working order. There were no signs of anything that would prevent the bell from ringing. How had she stopped the bell ringing, but left no trace?

THE GALAXY

The First National Museum in midtown Manhattan opened the autumn season with a special attraction – the world's third-largest emerald, called the "Galaxy", worth a king's ransom. The stone was placed in the centre room of the west wing with the tightest security the museum had ever seen.

Touching the crystal glass dome protecting the stone triggered audio and optical alarms. Steel shutters would lock all exits within four seconds. The showcase was supervized by closed-circuit television. In other words, robbery was unthinkable.

On opening day, visitors had to line up and were only admitted in groups of 45. Among the second group allowed in, one character caused considerable annoyance. He was obviously the worse for drink, staggering from room to room, always lagging behind the others.

The group had just left the centre room when all alarms went off. Within five seconds the security guards and a police officer arrived at the scene. The crystal glass dome was shattered and the man was lying on the floor in a drunken stupor. In his left hand he held the Galaxy. The whisky flask in his right hand was empty.

At the prison hospital, he was found to have an alcohol level five times over the limit. In due course he was given a two-year suspended sentence for wilful damage and disorderly conduct. When he left the courtroom, he was an extremely happy and richer man.

Why?

NELSON'S COLUMN

Rudolf Mueller from Dusseldorf arrived in London on his first trip abroad. He wanted to see as much as a four-day stay would permit and was particularly interested in famous sights, including the Tower of London, Madame Tussaud's, Trafalgar Square and Nelson's Column. Needless to say, he included Buckingham Palace and the Changing of the Guards in his plans.

Back at his hotel in Sussex Gardens, he studied all the tourist pamphlets to acquaint himself with the historical background. He read that the Tower of London was built in 1078 and that Nelson's Column was erected to celebrate the famous victory at Trafalgar, and that it was 170 feet high. This meant nothing to Rudolf as he was used to the metric system. Remembering from his school days that three feet equalled one yard, and that one yard was approximately equal to one metre, he pencilled in, next to a photograph of the column, 56 metres. Sadly, his inaccurate calculation cost the life of his best friend.

Explain.

#

WINTER TIME

A rich bachelor, living in a 10-room apartment in Manhattan, had a clock in every room. One Saturday evening in October he reset all the clocks for winter time before going to bed. Next morning he discovered that only two clocks showed the correct time.

Explain.

#

THE CHAIRS

Richard Madeley moved back into his family home, a run-down Georgian mansion in Windsor, after the death of his father, being the only remaining member of his family and therefore the sole heir to the estate.

As he had not lived in the house since his parents had divorced when he was a child, he went on a tour of the premises. During the tour, Richard discovered a locked room. He managed to force the door and found among the contents a set of six very beautiful chairs. On inspection Richard guessed that they were probably eighteenth century. The oak frames were in excellent condition but the chairs badly needed upholstering.

The following day, Richard telephoned a local upholsterer to come and look at the chairs. After inspecting them, the upholsterer quoted a price of £20 each for the work. Richard could not afford to have all six chairs re-covered at that price, but decided to have three done, and maybe later, when his finances picked up, the remaining three could be repaired.

Two weeks later, the upholsterer delivered the newly upholstered chairs. They looked exquisite. As Richard paid the upholsterer the sum agreed, the man said, "They look so beautiful, you must have the other three done." "I wish I could, but money is very tight," replied Richard. "Look, I'll make you a deal," responded the upholsterer. "I'll do the other three chairs for half the price of the first three." As Richard considered the offer, the upholsterer seemed to grow agitated. "OK, I'll do them for £50 each."

How could Richard refuse such an offer? He agreed and the upholsterer immediately loaded the remaining chairs on to his van and drove away. Richard watched the van disappear down the road and suddenly a look of dreadful realization crossed his face.

Explain.

CAN OF PEAS

A man walked into a shop and asked for a can of peas. "That will be $1, please," said the assistant, handing him the can. The man took the can, looked at it and said, "No, I said peas, not peaches." The assistant took back the can, read the label and handed it back to the man. "They are definitely peas, sir, look at the label." The man picked up the can, shook it and listened, "No, they are definitely peaches."

The assistant was beginning to get rather angry: "Perhaps you have a vision problem, because the label is quite clear. Even the illustration shows it. The contents are peas." "I'm afraid I do not like your tone of voice," replied the man, "may I, please, see the manager."

The assistant went to get the manager and on their approach the manager, with a condescending smile on his face, asked the man what the problem was. "Your assistant states that the contents of this can is peas, but I can assure you they are peaches. He has been very rude to me and I demand this can be opened to show that I am right, after which an apology is in order. "

The can was opened and sure enough, it contained peaches. The assistant and manager were completely flabbergasted. The manager offered the man $10 and an abject apology from the assistant. The man accepted the money and the apology, then left the shop.

Find an explanation.

THE LOPSIDED COINS

My friend Carlos is a collector of the paraphernalia which are the working tools of cardsharps, professional con artists and the like, people who prey on compulsive but unsophisticated gamblers for rich pickings. The items include marked cards, loaded dice and coins which have a bias toward heads or tails.

It was the latter which was the subject of animated discussion between Carlos and myself. We wondered whether, in full knowledge of the bias, we could use the coins for a game of "heads or tails?" which would be fair to both players. There are two coins involved, one biased toward heads and the other, precisely to the same degree, toward tails. Can you suggest a procedure which would give two gamblers an equal chance on flipping the coins?

THE DOWRY

While in primitive societies it is usually the husband who makes payment to the father-in-law, it is the custom in many western cultures for the son-in-law to receive a valuable dowry commensurate with the financial position of the bride's father. Rudolf Von Der Hagen, the youngest descendant of impoverished German nobility, intended to marry the daughter of Otto Wernicke, the banker. When Rudolf asked for her hand in marriage, Otto agreed to provide by way of dowry a luxury flat in Berlin, a reasonable annuity and a cash settlement of not less than £100,000.

After the wedding Wernicke handed Rudolf the deeds to the property, the insurance annuity certificate and an envelope. When Von Der Hagen opened the envelope, expecting a cheque or a government bond for £100,000, all he found was a torn piece of paper. While Rudolf was at first extremely angry, he shrugged his shoulders and seemed to accept the position.

Explain.

ANSWERS

01 MYOPIA

The piece of paper was a receipt from an optician for contact lenses, which Albert Grey had purchased before his return trip and was wearing at the time of the accident.

02 THE TELEPHONE CONVERSATION

A father and his child, or a paternal uncle or aunt and his/her nephew or niece.

03 THE MENU

The couple are regular customers on their way to a show, who have ordered an after-theatre dinner.

04 DISCERNING SHOPPER

She is a store employee. Part of her job is to remove items which will have gone beyond their "sell-by" date when the store opens the following morning.

05 PERIL IN THE AIR

A window shattered and the passenger was sucked out of the plane.

06 THE VERDICT

The trial took place in Scotland and the jury's verdict had been "Not Proven".

07 THE VANDAL

The restaurant owner had a slot machine installed on his premises by a criminal gang. A rival mob had forced him to install one of their machines, with guaranteed protection. When the original gang heard of the second machine they sent one of their heavies along to smash it up. After he left, the restaurant owner called the mob and told them what had happened, whereupon they eliminated the heavy.

08 JEALOUSY

The flying trapeze act required split-second precision to avoid an accident. The cue was provided by the band conducted by Arthur playing the "Minute Waltz" by Chopin and the trapeze exchange was to take place at the last note precisely. All Arthur had to do was to speed up the music by a mere one or two seconds.

09 THE ROBBERS

The "knowing" robber is in the habit of listening to his
Walkman and, during jobs, tunes in to the local police-calls
station. Through the earphones, he had heard a police car
being dispatched to the scene to investigate.

10 THE CAREFUL DRIVER

I was travelling in the wrong direction down a one-way street;
the cars I passed were all going the other way.

11 THE MASK

The man is a deep-sea diver. A diver at great depth can be
affected by a phenomenon commonly referred to as "rapture of
the deep". This condition causes euphoria, and the afflicted loses
his grasp on reality and becomes convinced that equipment, such
as the face mask, is useless and should be discarded.

12 THE ANTIQUE CANDELABRUM

The distinguished-looking man appeared to be an expert on
seventeenth-century works of art and immediately recognized
the candelabrum as the work of Giovanni Lorenzo Bernini. He
knew it was one of a pair, and he wanted to buy the pair. He was
most disappointed to hear that only one was available, and he
mentioned that he was prepared to pay £25,000 for the set but
that one piece was of no interest.

Eventually he was persuaded by the antiques dealer to buy the one piece for £5,000, while repeating his offer of £20,000 for the second piece to complete the set. The dealer, most anxious not to lose the deal, phones round the trade without success until, two days later, he hears from a colleague that the second candelabrum has indeed been offered.

When Robert shows the piece to the dealer, he recognizes this to be the genuine article and is glad to pay £9,000 for it. Needless to say, the distinguished-looking gentleman could no longer be located.

13 MASS MURDER?

The man was a lighthouse keeper and those who died were sailors shipwrecked as a result of the lighthouse light having been switched off.

14 THE ENDURANCE TEST

Hans Mueller was obviously cheating. It is impossible to perspire after spending five days in the desert with only half a litre of water as by then he would have been severely dehydrated.

15 THE CAT

Brian Lewis pointed out that his whole face was deeply, uniformly and genuinely tanned, which would not be the case if he had worn a beard.

16 THE BARBER'S SHOP

David regularly has assignations with the barber's wife and wants to ascertain how soon the barber is likely to come home.

17 THE EXPERIMENT

The man was Alexander Fleming, who in 1929 prepared a culture plate of staphylococcus as part of his research programme. The culture was unexpectedly contaminated by spores of *Penicillium notatum*. The colonies of staphylococcus disintegrated into a mould. Fleming was sufficiently intrigued to isolate the mould in pure culture. This was found to be a substance which had a powerful destructive effect on many bacteria. The first antibiotic had been discovered.

18 SMART KID

Let us call the experts Mr White and Mr Black, according to the colour of the pieces each played against my daughter. Mr White played first. My daughter copied his first move as her opening against Mr Black at the other board. When Mr Black answered this move, she copied his move at the first board as her reply to Mr White, and so on. In this way the simultaneous games against the two experts became a single game between them; my daughter merely served as a messenger to transmit the moves.

Hence she was certain to either win one game and lose the other or draw both, bettering my showing.

19 GAME-SET-MATCH

A brook was running alongside the North end of the tennis court, and had Ernest played South many of his balls would have landed in the water, particularly as a strong breeze was blowing in the same direction.

20 THE ROLLS-ROYCE CORNICHE

Ronnie Breskal is a film star and Ernesto Saler his stand-in stuntman. They were filming a scene for their latest adventure movie.

21 LAST LETTER

She was a skywriter. Lightning struck her plane and she crashed.

22 DAILY ROUTINE

Joe is blind but he has an arrangement with a shop assistant in the store to guide him across the busy street.

23 SUICIDE

Henry and Ann were obviously murdered, as the purported suicide note was grammatically incorrect. It should have read: " – Ann and me." A philologist would not have made the mistake.

24 THE KANGAROO COURT

Hans was an undercover agent for the special anti-terrorist unit and had succeeded in infiltrating the cell. When the official was kidnapped and sentenced, Helldorf volunteered to perform the execution in order to save the man's life. He shot him with blanks; the blood was a "special effects" exercise with the props supplied by Hans. The press was misled by the police to avoid blowing Helldorf's cover.

25 DRINK-DRIVE

The man was acting as a decoy to draw the policemen away from the club, whose members – some of whom were more than slightly inebriated – drove off in a hurry as soon as the coast was clear.

26 THE TWO SOLICITORS

Smith's full name was Tracy Smith. Jones had started an affair with Tracy, claiming that he was a bachelor, and he had promised to marry her.

27 ALL SYSTEMS GO!

Rockets are launched in the direction of the earth's rotation, from West to East. To take advantage of the maximum "push" from the earth, launch sites are located as close to the equator as possible.

28 COPACABANA

Inspector Garcia had noticed that Gert had a white mark on his ring finger, whereas his arm was uniformly tanned and showed no mark where the Rolex had supposedly been.

29 THE MOUNTAIN

The border between Turkey and Iraq runs across the mountain, with the peak being on the Iraqi side.

80 PLANE CRASH

Alfie Huberman's Piper Apache was a remote-controlled model.

81 STRANGERS ON A TRAIN

The man was a TV celebrity; the woman was a deaf mute. Because the man was chewing gum, she assumed he was saying something to her and gave him the paper and pen to write her a note. He assumed she was asking for his autograph and signed the paper. As his signature meant nothing to her, she threw the paper away when she got off the train.

82 TWIN BROTHER

Kurt Wilton was wrong. His twin brother was also a registered civil engineer in California, who had a twin brother.

83 THE COMPETITORS

Steve was determined to prove that his company was more successful than its competitors in promoting a product. To achieve this he conspired with the team filming the commercial to introduce subliminal sequences denigrating Brand "X". Subliminal advertising, transmitted below one's conscious threshold, is designed to manipulate the viewer's mind. It has been tried in the USA, but declared illegal. Mike had been suspicious and had freeze-framed the Brand "Y" commercial, revealing a subliminal message to the detriment of Brand "X".

84 A JOB IN A MILLION

Robert Bradley is chief steward in the first-class section, working for a world-famous airline.

85 THE PARIS FAIR

Paul had been taken ill during the night and it was discovered that he had typhoid. So as not to cause panic and jeopardize the World's Fair, the hotel management had arranged for him to be taken to an isolation hospital run by nuns and had sealed Room 13 to conceal the fact that Paul had ever arrived. (A true story, and the subject of a book and a movie.)

86 MARITAL PROBLEM

Jason and Dean were both clergymen. Dean married Jason to Denise, which explains why they share the same wedding anniversary. Jason married Jackie to a man whose name happens to be Peter. On another occasion, John married Dean to a girl called Paula.

87 POLAR EXPEDITION

Celsius or Fahrenheit makes no difference. To convert Celsius to Fahrenheit, multiply by 9, divide by 5 and add 32°. Thus:
$-40°C = (-40 \times 9/5 + 32°F) = -40°F$

88 UPSIDE DOWN

The man was the subject of an experiment conducted by scientists in Germany in the mid-1920s.

The human eye in its function can be compared to a camera: the photographic lens is represented by the cornea and lens of the eye, and the photosensitive screen of the camera corresponds to the retina. As in a camera, the refracted rays form an image on the retina which is much smaller than the object being viewed and is symmetrically inverted. The human brain corrects the inversion by turning the retina image upside down. To test the mechanics of this double-take, a group of ophthalmologists fitted several test subjects with special spectacles, which had the effect of turning images around. It took only a few hours until the brain compensated and the world appeared normal again. In reverse the same thing happened – after removal of the special spectacles the images appeared upside down until the brain had made the adjustment once again.

The man in the puzzle had these spectacles removed before starting to walk, and the experiment was to establish the time-lag for correcting the image.

89 POLICE EMERGENCY

The second police car had stalled in a tunnel so was unable to receive radio messages. They had therefore not heard the call for backup from the police station.

40 WHAT AM I?

A dream.

41 ROUGE ET NOIR

Each time Philip bets 500 francs on red, Deborah places 500 francs on black. Because of zero, they lose their stake about once in every 74 throws, but Deborah accepts this modest loss. The activity keeps her husband happy and they both enjoy the exciting ambiance of the casino.

42 THE MOTOR POOL

Sunlight operates a merry-go-round at the Prater, a well-known permanent fun-fair in Vienna. The cars, which have a width tyre-to-tyre of one metre, travel round a circle with a radius of 10 metres. Consequently the outer tyres cover a distance 10 per cent longer than the inner tyres.

43 BANK ROBBERY

The manager's assistant, in collusion with the cleaner, had taken a photograph of the safe, which had been blown up to life-size. This was placed in front of the safe so that the guard could see only what he thought was the intact safe door. The cleaner removed the photograph when she arrived at the bank on Monday morning and disposed of it before anyone else arrived.

44 EXHIBIT "A"

The murder was committed by a left-handed man. The accused had strenuously denied being left-handed, and as he was ambidextrous to some extent he could write with his right hand. However, he instinctively caught the knife with his left hand, which gave him away.

45 THE ODD SOCK

One of the passengers turned round and exclaimed with a serious face: "I can see somebody is travelling light!"

46 SECRETS OF THE LAKE

The children had not drowned. Madeleine had taken them to a friend across the lake, in whom she had confided. Madeleine had hoped that her desperate charade would make Rene realize what might have happened and terminate the affair. Madeleine could have been indicted for making a false report and wasting the time of the police, but in view of the circumstances she was not charged.

47 THE FATAL BULLET

Faced with Mario's reluctance, the boss of all bosses hired a contract killer, who had shot Sylvia several hours before Mario's bullet. A post-mortem found that it was the first shot that killed Sylvia.

When Mario entered the apartment, Sylvia was not asleep, but dead. As there is no law against shooting a corpse, Mario had to be released.

48 THE CHAPEL

Mont St. Michel in Normandy, France, is a tidal island, cut off from the mainland at certain high tides. Henry had forgotten to enquire when the next one was due before setting out on his pilgrimage.

49 SALE OF THE YEAR

This is what the note said: "I have a severe case of laryngitis, and on doctor's orders I must not speak as it could be dangerous in my condition. However, I am the manager and if you don't let me go to the front, I will not open the store."

50 THE DAGGER

When the telephone receiver was checked for fingerprints only Maynard's were found, but not the nephew's. There was no reason why Albert should have worn gloves unless he was the killer. He was careless in not taking the gloves off before dialling 999.

51 THE CAR CRASH

The surgeon was Robert Jones' mother.

52 PERIL IN THE SKY

As Richard jumped, the left leg of his nylon suit was caught up in a loose screw on the door frame. He was unable to extricate himself and was kept dangling in mid-air. He did not dare to pull the ripcord, as opening the parachute would almost certainly have killed him. The drag would have smashed him against the plane's fuselage at about 100 miles per hour. There was no way of warning the pilot as in those days the old Dakotas were not radio-equipped. When the plane landed, Richard was dragged along the airfield. However, the parachute pack took the brunt of the impact and abrasion.

53 THE CADILLAC

The Customs men would also have found flour in the spare tyre and in the false bottoms of the suitcases. The New York drug barons had long suspected that one of their gang was an informant or an undercover agent. Different operators hid what were supposed to be drugs in the various hiding places. As the enforcement agents pounced on the door panels, they inadvertently identified the informant.

54 SPRING IN THE MOUNTAINS

The couple had been walking in the mountains during the winter when they were hit by an avalanche and buried. In the spring, when the snow had melted, their bodies were exposed.

55 THE SHOPPING MALL

Herbert was following his own theory and was waiting for
Harriet in the bookshop. His general strategy needs to be
improved by identifying who should stay put.

56 THE SLOW HORSES

Switch horses!

57 PILOT ERROR

Tim had served in the Royal Air Force for 18 years and, after
leaving, had decided to apply for a position as a commercial
airline pilot. He had been training in a 747 flight simulator, and
went on to become a fully fledged British Airways pilot.

58 THE VENTURE

The two men were trying an Atlantic balloon crossing from New
York to London, which was heavily sponsored by a multi-national
corporation. A sudden gust was blowing them toward a sky-
scraper. A collision might have shattered their cabin, so to get a
quick lift they had to jettison some of their sand-bag ballasts.

59 PRESUMPTION OF AUTHORITY

The witness was the bank clerk who gave the description of the impostor to the police. By a fortunate coincidence he saw the man and Dawson sitting together in a restaurant the day before the hearing.

60 MERCADO INC.

Harry Green discovered that Holt had defrauded the company over a number of years of more than $1 million. His first impulse was to prefer criminal charges, but on second thoughts he realized that he was unlikely to recover the funds and his company could not stand the loss. He therefore conspired with Conrad Holt to concoct the kidnapping story. This seemed the ideal solution, as Holt escaped a prison sentence while Mercado was saved from bankruptcy. After hearing of Holt's death, Green was afraid that there were papers that would reveal his part in the conspiracy.

61 BUREAU DE CHANGE

Tim intended to hold up the bank and he was casing the job.

62 EAT AND YOU DIE

Eve gave Adam the apple in the Garden of Eden and he became mortal as a consequence.

63 THE JUDGEMENT

The man was one of Siamese twins.

64 DEAL OF THE YEAR

In fact, Frank Forrester saw an advertisement offering a list of number plates including DEM 10 with N as the year of registration. In other words, the plate read DEM1ON. As this was the somewhat unusual first name of Miller's wife, he knew that Bruce, in his snobbishness, would go for it and pay any price. The new owner was prepared to pay a top market price for the car, but the number plate meant nothing to him.

65 LOADED GUN

The defendant was in fact not guilty. As stated, he had put the gun in the right-hand pocket of his overcoat. It was a reversible coat, however, and when it started to rain, he reversed the coat, thereby switching the gun from outside right to inside left.

66 RESEMBLANCE

Peter's school friend was Lucy's mother, who had become a QC and married the headmaster of the French Lycée.

67 THE PROFESSOR

The girl looked up at the Professor with a condescending smile, took his hand, and said: "Don't be silly, Daddy. Come, I take you home."

68 STRANGE BEHAVIOUR

This, but for some details, is a true story. Gerald Watson was in fact John Stonehouse, a Labour Member of Parliament and former Minister (1969 – 1970). He had run into severe business problems in connection with a Bangladesh bank he helped to found and, to escape from it all, he decided to change his identity.

Stonehouse adopted the idea described in Frederic Forsyth's book, The Day of the Jackal, and obtained a passport in the name of a dead man – Joe Markham. He entered the US at Miami as John Stonehouse, but just after passing Immigration he pretended to have left some hand luggage on the plane and was allowed out. He passed through Immigration again a little later, using his Markham passport, then booked in at the Fontainebleau Hotel, Miami Beach.

On the morning on which Stonehouse was to disappear forever, he left the key with the hall porter. The sea was calm and the beach deserted. He swam to the Doral and emerged as Joe Markham. After he left for Australia, the US Immigration records showed that John Stonehouse had entered but not left, which confirmed the assumption that he had drowned. The rest is history.

69 THE UNFAITHFUL WIFE

On Eva's way out, John had noticed a ladder in her left stocking. When she went to the kitchen for coffee, he noticed that the ladder was now on her right leg.

70 WOLF AMONG THE SHEEP

The wolf squeezed through the bars, killed as many sheep as he thought necessary, tore them into small pieces and pushed them through the bars. He followed through and ate his fill at leisure outside the compound. Some time later, in a Mensa IQ test, the wolf scored 161.

71 THE BESTSELLER

Victor Bronson was blind and was reading from the Braille manuscript of the novel.

72 THE MAGNA CARTA

Eric and his friend were freelance journalists who wanted to penetrate the security system and use the venture as a syndicated feature for the media.

As a safeguard, Eric had written to the Director of Public Prosecutions (DPP) describing the proposed operation as an exercise in investigative journalism. It was the DPP who was killed in the accident, and his briefcase with the letter – which would have exonerated Eric – was burnt to ashes in the fire.

73 DEAL A BRIDGE HAND

Andrew dealt the bottom card to himself, then continued dealing from the bottom counter-clockwise.

74 ENIGMATIC DIALOGUE

The piece of paper pushed across the counter demanded, "Hand over all the money you have in the till or my partner, who is in your house, will kill your children." As an afterthought, he said, "No fifties," as he suspected their numbers were recorded to make them traceable.

Before he left, Tom heard him say to Elsa, "Close the bank and both of you stay another hour. If you phone the police before the time is up, your kids are dead."

75 WITNESSES FOR THE DEFENCE

Bruce and Harry both had monozygotic (identical) twins and their defence lawyer had called their respective brothers. All four brothers denied committing the robbery, and as the prosecution could not ascertain which pair of twins had actually committed the crime, the jury was forced to return a verdict of not guilty.

76 THE ORDINANCE

The barber was the wife of the Mayor.

77 IRA JUSTICE

The man had artificial legs and was therefore unhurt. He had only pretended to be in pain to allay suspicion – and likely additional shots to more vulnerable parts of his anatomy.

78 ROBBERY SUSPECT

Detective Roberts knew that deceased people are not buried in New Orleans because the ground is too wet, but are placed in mausoleums or cremated.

79 NUISANCE CALLS

No, the police were not outwitted. They opened the coin box, collected a few coins from the top of the heap and soon established that two of them matched the man's fingerprints.

80 DOUBLE HOMICIDE

The murderer was a forensic pathologist who lifted the fingerprints of a dead man on whom he had performed an autopsy and transferred them to the murder weapon. The corpse was then cremated, as per the family's wishes.

81 THE PRESIDENTS

If the fifth US president was not among those who died on that date, the newspaper item would almost certainly have made the more impressive statement that, "Three of the first four presidents of the United States died on July 4th." Therefore, Tom was certain that the fifth president, James Monroe, died on that date.

82 THE PHONE-IN

The moderator had just announced, "We are now contacting Mr and Mrs Bradley of Alperton for their views." Tom heard the ringing tone and, much to his surprise, a man answered the phone. Tom recognized the voice as that of his friend Michael, whom he had suspected of having an affair with his wife.

83 THE SHARPSHOOTER

The sharpshooter's hat was hung over the end of his gun.

84 THE X-RAY FILM

In his younger days Robert Blocker suffered a compound fracture in one of his legs while skiing in Scotland. The bone pieces had to be fastened together with metal rods and plates. The security detector checks at the airports would be set off every time he passed them, and the x-ray films were needed to explain the reason.

85 THE EXHUMATION

Geoffrey Griffiths was being blackmailed by the man in the coffin. The amounts demanded increased each time until Griffiths could bear it no longer. When the blackmailer visited him to negotiate a large final payment against the surrender of the incriminating document, the undertaker pretended to agree and offered him a drink in celebration, laced with arsenic. After his death the problem of disposing of the body arose. Griffiths found what he thought was the perfect solution, which would have been successful but for a quirk of fate.

86 BABY-MINDER

The whole incident had been set up and filmed by the Candid Camera crew for their new TV series.

87 OVERHEARD

The operative word is "can", as in "tin can", and the solution is therefore self-evident.

88 JILTED BRIDE

She had jammed the clapper with packed snow, which melted during the ceremony. No one noticed the damp patch below the bell.

89 THE GALAXY

The emerald the man was found clutching was a superb replica. He had swallowed the real gem and then emptied the flask of whisky. Before he smashed the crystal dome, he had been faking being inebriated, but after he had drunk the contents of his hip flask, and by the time he was examined in the prison hospital, his blood-alcohol level had risen very high.

90 NELSON'S COLUMN

Rudolf's friend had decided to bungee jump from the top of Nelson's Column and had asked for the height so that he could arrange the correct length of elastic cord. Rudolf's miscalculation meant that his friend's rope was too long, thereby causing his death.

91 WINTER TIME

Eight clocks ran on house electricity. During the night there was a power cut, or outage, which affected these clocks but not the other two, which were wound up or battery-operated.

92 THE CHAIRS

The upholsterer had discovered that gold coins were hidden in each of the first three chairs and he was obviously eager to get his hands on the remaining three chairs and their contents.

93 CAN OF PEAS

The man was an inveterate practical joker and had a can of peaches in his bag with an identical label to the peas' can, which he had switched after a previous purchase. When the assistant went to get the manager, the man replaced the genuine can of peas with the fake can.

94 THE LOPSIDED COINS

There are probably several ways in which an equal chance could be achieved. Since the coins are biased, the outcome of tossing one coin is obviously inequitable, but flipping both coins can result in:

Coin 1	Coin 2	
Heads	Heads	(HH)
Tails	Tails	(TT)
Heads	Tails	(HT)
Tails	Heads	(TH)

As HH is as equally likely to come up as TT, this could form the basis of a wager, whereby a flip producing HT and TH should be ignored.

Another solution would be to glue the two coins together in such a way that the biased faces are either touching or are at the outside of the fused coins, in which case the bias is eliminated by counterbalance.

95 THE DOWRY

Rudolf Von Der Hagen was a notorious gambler heavily in debt to the local casino. Otto Wernicke had purchased his IOU, torn it up and placed it in the envelope, thus enabling Rudolf to start his marriage with a clean slate.

ACKNOWLEDGEMENTS

Sources for this type of puzzle are relatively rare and offer insufficient material to fill a book of this size. Consequently many "Strange Situations" had to be invented and I spent many sleepless nights racking my brains. I also became a scourge to friends and relatives cajoling them to contribute.

The response was less than overwhelming, though I should be grateful for small mercies. In addition, I am indebted to the following authors and/or publishers whose material I have used in its original form, or whose ideas have provided me with raw material for some of the "Hidden Evidence" stories I have constructed: Victor Serebriakoff – *A Mensa Puzzle Book*; Scot Morris – Omni Games; Martin Gardner; P. Carter & K. Russell; Eugene P. Northrop; and Gyles Brandreth.

Les Smith assisted in producing original ideas and being the devil's advocate in criticizing puzzles of my own construction. Jennifer Iles coped most efficiently with numerous changes and revisions.